ULTIMATE TOY COLLECTOR SHOPKINS!

Mary Boone with Amy Bizzarri

TRIUMPH BOOKS

This book is available in quantity at special discounts for your group or organization. For further information, contact:

Triumph Books LLC
814 North Franklin Street
Chicago, Illinois 60610
(312) 337–0747
www.triumphbooks.com

Printed in U.S.A.
ISBN: 978-1-62937-179-5
Content developed and packaged by Rockett Media, Inc.
Written by Mary Boone with Amy Bizzarri
Edited by Bob Baker
Design and page production by Patricia Frey
Cover design by Patricia Frey
Photography by Cait Lin Foto

contents

introduction

Do you remember your first mini-figurine collection? When I was a little girl, I collected Smurfs, small blue creatures who lived in mushroom-shaped homes. Today, I love seeing my 5-year-old daughter, Chiara, delight in her Shopkins collection. Collecting toys is a hobby that offers hours of fun. Trading toys with friends, thinking of creative new ways to display your collection, and seeing your collection grow are some of the unforgettable joys of childhood.

Shopkins might be little in size but they bring big smiles to people's faces! These colorful, cute and tiny characters are inspired by the everyday items you can find in your local grocery store. I share the secret joy when you open up the latest blind bag, hoping to reveal an ultra-rare, glittery Shopkin. You can set up a grocery store of your very own, where funny little Shopkins line the shelves: Dippy Avocado, Chloe Flower and Juicy Orange keep the fruit and vegetable department bright and cheery. Chee Zee and Spilt Milk bring their silly smiles to the dairy aisle. Waffle Sue, Minnie-Minty and Ice Cream Dream make us hungry for dessert!

And since the Shopkins family keeps growing and growing - with Season Two bringing the tally up to over 150 new characters - the fun is just getting started! I just keep hoping to find a glittery Cupcake Queen! From secretly carrying them around with you at school or play, to creating your own Shopkins video, to hosting a Shopkins-themed party, there is so much you can do with your Shopkins collection. So grab your favorite Shopkins and get ready to have a blast as you grow your sweet and cheerful collection!

amy

"Super Shopkins Fan"

CHAPTER ONE

Shopkins Take the Toy World by Storm

One of the biggest toys in the world right now is so small you can fit a couple of them in your hand.

Shopkins are itty-bitty, super cute grocery-themed characters that have stolen the hearts of kids — and adults — all over the world.

Moose Toys, a company based in Melbourne, Australia, first introduced Shopkins in July 2014 with 150 different collectibles. At the same time, they began to release very short online videos featuring the Shopkins world. Those videos helped spread the Shopkins love in a big way. By February 2015, a dozen videos had been posted on Shopkins' official YouTube channel; those videos had been viewed 26.2 million times.

Working with Toys

From toy inventors to store clerks, the toy industry supports approximately 618,350 full-time jobs in the United States.

Kids have fallen in love with Shopkins. In fact, the tiny, colorful toys were such an instant hit that they began to sell out in stores nationwide within a matter of weeks and online in as little as 24 hours. A second series of the miniatures was released in November 2014.

Shopkins come packaged with a shopping bag or shopping basket, which can be used to carry the characters. All packs of Shopkins come with at least one character you cannot see before you purchase. With the 12-pack, for example, kids can see 10 of the Shopkins in the package, along with four shopping bags and a basket, but inside the basket are two blind-packed characters. This packaging technique adds to the fun of collecting – and opening – the toys.

All Shopkins are grouped into "teams" by their location in the grocery store; categories include fruits and vegetables, dairy, bakery, sweet treats, party food, frozen foods and health and beauty. Beyond individual characters, children can add to their collections with a shopping cart that holds up to 60 Shopkins, or playsets such as the Fruit & Veg Stand, So Cool Fridge and Spin Mix Baking Stand.

Shopkins are obviously popular with kids, but adults also are beginning to see how great they are. The Toy Industry Association of America named Shopkins a finalist for one of its 2014 Toy of the Year Awards. The toy review site TTPM.com named Shopkins to its 2014 Holiday Most Wanted List, while Toy Insider, a website specializing in toy news and reviews, named Shopkins to its "Hot 20" list for 2014.

"We know that girls love all things miniature, so we created these cute collectible characters with intricate detailing,"

I Want to Design Toys

Designing toys sounds like fun, but it's actually a lot of hard work.

Toy designers often start projects by sketching ideas. They may draw hundreds of ideas before they land upon one they want to actually develop. Once the designers have a concept they like, they will design a prototype of the toy. A prototype is a model of the toy. It shows how the toy looks and moves, how durable it is, and what materials it's made of. At this stage, when the toy can actually be held and operated, is a good time to make sure that it's safe. If the prototype doesn't work the way the designer intended, they may adjust their plans and create another prototype.

When the designers have a prototype they're happy with, they can try to sell their idea to a toy manufacturer.

Many toy designers specialize in a certain type of toy. For example, one designer might make dolls while another focuses on educational games or puzzles.

Many toy designers go to college to study art, industrial design or engineering. There are a handful of U.S. colleges and universities that offer special degrees or certifications in toy design, including the Fashion Institute of Technology in New York City and Otis College of Art and Design in Los Angeles. If you think you might like to become a toy designer, you'll want to work extra hard in your math, science, English and art classes. Of course, creativity is another very important job requirement.

Yes, toy designers do get to play on the job and they get to make kids happy. If those are things you think you'd enjoy, maybe you should become a toy designer when you grow up!

Oldest Toy

The National Toy Hall of Fame has recognized The Stick as the world's oldest toy, noting that sticks can turn into swords, magic wands, fishing poles and light sabers. Children build with sticks, bat balls with them, and walk with them. They are the original building blocks for creative play. Go play with a stick!

Paul Solomon, co-Chief Executive Officer of Moose Toys said in a news release.

Christopher Byrne, a respected toy industry expert and writer for TTPM, said miniature collectibles have long been popular with boys. "Moose (Toys) has adapted that play pattern for girls with the same level of imagination, innovation and great design that resonates with the type of play to which girls typically gravitate," he said, adding that Shopkins is consistently trending on TTPM as one of the most popular new toys the site has reviewed.

Beyond being adorable, there are a handful of obvious reasons for Shopkins' popularity:

They're affordable. A set of two Shopkins characters in a tiny shopping basket retails for $2.99 to $3.29. Even the most elaborate of playsets sells for approximately $20.

They're fun. Based upon real foods (Apple Blossom, Bread Head, Pret-Zelle), health and beauty supplies (Lippy Lips, Polly Polish) housewares (Lana Lamp, Brenda Blenda) and more, these toys run on imagination rather than batteries.

They're collectable. Each pack of Shopkins comes with a collector's guide that looks like a shopping list. The guides list each available character so you can look for new "groceries" to check off the shopping list. In addition to "Common" Shopkins which are simply fun to play with, there are also "Exclusive," "Rare," "Limited Edition," "Special Edition" and "Ultra Rare" characters.

All in all, these tiny figurines are packed with enormous fun, making them a giant hit with kids of all ages, all over the world.

Big Business

The average price of a toy in the United States is around $9. According to the Toy Industry Association, more than 3 billion toys are sold across the country each year for a total of approximately $22 billion.

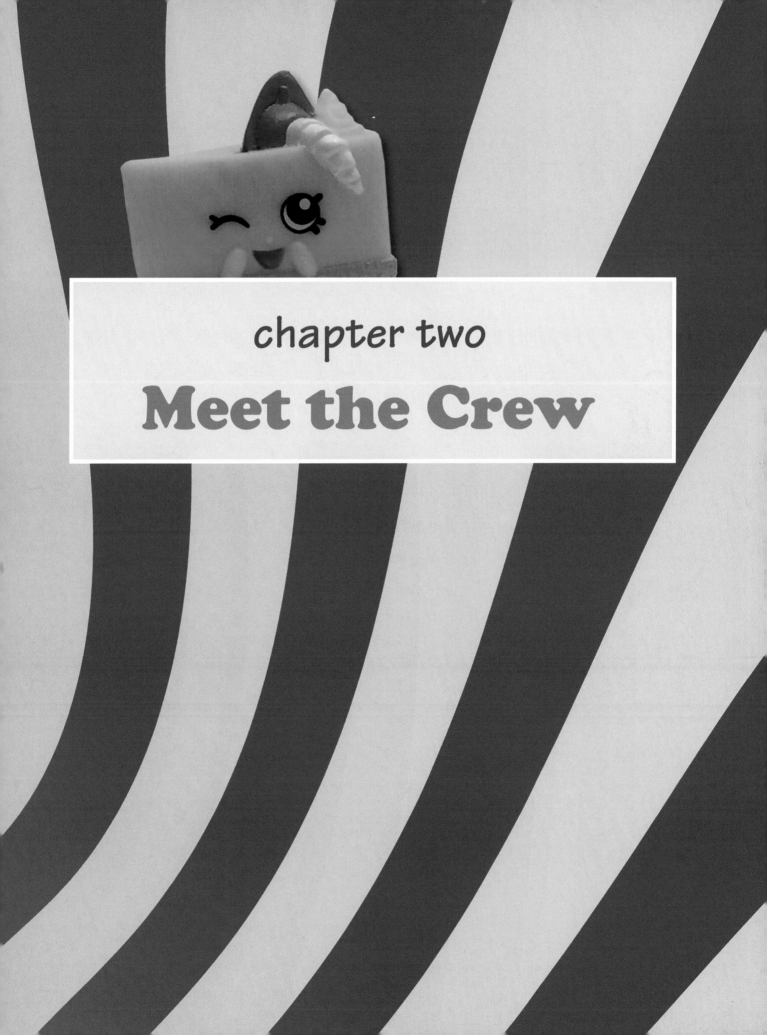

chapter two
Meet the Crew

At first glance, Shopkins look like any other toy. But those who have gotten to know this cast of pint-sized grocery-themed characters know that they're actually quite spectacular.

Lori Pace wrote about her love for Shopkins in her blog, "A Day in Motherhood." The Houston, Texas, mom of three said she rarely gets excited about new toys anymore, but she fell in love with Shopkins for a handful of reasons:

★ They are original.

★ Boys and girls can play with them.

★ They promote group play.

★ They promote creativity.

★ They are affordable.

"So many toys come into this house and are cast aside in a matter of minutes," Pace wrote. "Shopkins really has stood the test of time and the creativity I am watching while (my daughters) and their friends play with them, is awesome!"

Rebecca English, a mother from West Midlands, England, wrote a glowing review of Shopkins in her blog "Here Come

the Girls," noting that her three daughters have enjoyed playing together with their Shopkins.

"Whoever invented this toy was a genius because it kept them so happy for hours," she said. "The thing I like the best is that Shopkins complement any other toy. You can use any small dolls and character figures with the (play) set and get them to go shopping and push the trolley."

California mom Jessamine Dungo, who writes a blog called "My Great Finds," appreciates that collecting Shopkins has led her two daughters to become more organized as they develop systems for sorting and storing the tiny toys. Another benefit: the toys are helping to improve her daughters' memorization skills.

"I honestly don't know most of the Shopkins' names, but my 3-year-old daughter does," she wrote. "I am surprised that she knows almost all of the Shopkins' names!"

It's nice that adults think Shopkins are cool but it's even more important that kids like them.

It's nice that adults think Shopkins are cool but it's even more important that kids like them. And, boy, do they like them! Boys and girls, ages 5 and up, are drawn to the character's funny names, spunky personalities and vibrant designs. While it's impossible to introduce readers to the entire gang, here's a primer on a dozen of our favorite Shopkins. Enjoy!

Al Foils

Season: Two
ID: 2-074
Rarity: Common
Finish: Classic
Favorite hobby: Wrapping with friends.
Shopkins BFF: Soda Pops
Hang Out: Pantry

Bread Head

Season: One
ID: 1-033
Rarity: Common
Finish: Classic
Favorite hobby: Chatting on the phone.
Shopkins BFF: Kooky Cookie
Hang out: Bakery

Hanging with Shopkins

Chee Zee

Season: One

ID: 1-065

Rarity: Common

Finish: Classic

Favorite hobby: Rapping with my BFFs.

Shopkins BFFs: Cheezey-B and Freezy Peazy

Hang out: Dairy Case

Cornell Mustard

Season: Two

ID: 2-076

Rarity: Common

Finish: Classic

Favorite hobby: Solving mysteries.

Shopkins BFF: Bart Beans

Hang Out: Pantry

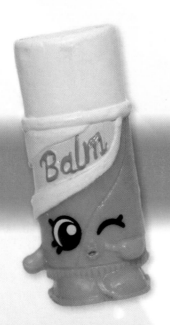

Dippy Avocado

Season: Two

ID: 2-015

Rarity: Common

Finish: Classic

Favorite hobby: Taking a dip on a hot day.

Shopkins BFFs: Silly Chilli and Brenda Blenda

Hang Out: Fruit and Veg

Gran Jam

Season: One

ID: 1-022

Rarity: Common

Finish: Classic

Favorite hobby: Knitting.

Shopkins BFF: Papa Tomato

Hang out: Pantry

Ice Cream Dream

Season: Two

ID: 2-058

Rarity: Common

Finish: Classic

Favorite hobby: Chilling out alone in her cone.

Shopkins BFF: Waffle Sue

Hang out: Sweet Treats

Miss Missy-Moo

Season: One

ID: 1-006

Rarity: Common

Finish: Classic

Favorite hobby: Making mud pies.

Shopkins BFF: Rockin' Broc

Hang out: Fruit and Veg

Silly Chilli

Season: Two

ID: 2-008

Rarity: Common

Finish: Classic

Favorite hobby: Eating very HOT dogs.

Shopkins BFF: Dippy Avocado

Hang out: Fruit and Veg

Swiss Miss

Season: One

ID: 1-066

Rarity: Common

Finish: Classic

Favorite hobby: Stand-up comedian.

Shopkins BFF: Tommy Ketchup

Hang out: Dairy Case

What Makes a Good Toy?

Toys come in all shapes and sizes. Whether they're plush or shiny metal, melodic or mobile, the very best toys stimulate the imagination and contribute to the development of a child's mental, physical, social and emotional skills.

The American Specialty Toy Retailing Association emphasizes these five characteristics of a good toy: play value, design, values, quality and appropriateness.

Shopkins have many of these characteristics and are especially great for "pretend play." That's a fancy way of saying there isn't a book or instruction manual that tells you exactly how to play with Shopkins. Instead, kids get to make up games, pretend they're having adventures and imagining conversations. The process of pretending builds skills in many important developmental areas such as learning about their likes and dislikes, learning to interact with others, and developing thinking strategies and communication skills.

The experts at the Illinois Early Learning Project also stress that good toys are:

★ Not violent.
★ Easy to clean and sanitize.
★ Safe, with no sharp edges. Additionally, small parts may present choking hazards for children under 3 years old.
★ Durable.
★ Attractive, with pleasing shapes, colors, design details, textures and sounds.
★ Appropriate to the child's age and abilities.
★ Interesting enough that a child will play with them over and over again.

Good toys engage children, encouraging them to think, learn, imagine, feel and ask questions. Above all, the best toys are fun! If a toy is boring or dull, it's simply not a good toy.

Tommy Ketchup

Season: One

ID: 1-015

Rarity: Common

Finish: Classic

Favorite hobby: Trolley riding

Shopkins BFF: Frank Furter

Hang out: Pantry

Wobbles

Season: One

ID: 1-083

Rarity: Common

Finish: Classic

Favorite hobby: Hip hop dancing.

Shopkins BFF: Snow Crush

Hang out: Party Food

Shopkins are cool

chapter three
Exclusive, Rare and Limited Edition

Let's start off by making it clear that all Shopkins are adorable. From Bread Head and Peppe Pepper to Sugar Lump and Melonie Pips, the vivid details on these teeny playthings make them undeniably appealing.

That said, most kids and collectors who are in-the-know have created lists of special Shopkins they'd love to add to their collections.

The vast majority of Shopkins are labeled "Common." That doesn't mean they're not special, it simply means they're the easiest to find and, after you've been collecting a while, you're likely to get repeats. Of all the Shopkins available in early 2015, 121 were labeled as "Common." That's why Shopkins aficionados are so excited when they score non-"Common" toys — there simply aren't as many of them. In fact, in early 2015, there were only 10 "Exclusive," 12 "Limited Edition," 71 "Rare," 32 "Special Edition" and 47 "Ultra Rare" Shopkins.

Because the most difficult-to-find Shopkins are hidden so you can't see them until you buy them, fans have taken to YouTube to look for clues. Some collectors suggest watching videos of "Limited Edition" or "Ultra Rare" reveals and then taking note of the "Common" Shopkins that are visible in those 5- or 12-packs. They say they've

Playsets

Four playsets are available to make playing with Shopkins even more fun. A favorite playset is the Small Mart. It includes a delivery chute, checkout stand with movable conveyor belt, cash register and shopping cart – just like a real supermarket, but more fun!

had success finding their most-wanted Shopkins when they purchase the exact packs they've seen in those clips.

While it's impossible to introduce readers to all these incredibly special Shopkins, here are a few of our favorites:

Angie Ankle Boot

Season: Two

ID: 2-142

Rarity: Limited Edition

Finish: Bling

Favorite hobby: Disco dancing.

Shopkins BFFs: Cute Boot

Hang out: Limited Edition

Oh, So Rare!

The rarest of all the Shopkins is Cupcake Queen! She has a metallic finish and can reportedly only be found in 5- and 12-packs.

Chloe Flower

Season: Two

ID: 2-001

Rarity: Rare

Finish: Classic

Favorite hobby: Leafing through the newspaper.

Shopkins BFF: Rockin' Broc

Hang out: Fruit and Veg

Cool Cube

Season: One

ID: 1-132

Rarity: Special Edition

Finish: Frozen

Favorite Hobby: Snowboarding, skiing, sledding and ice skating.

Shopkins BFF: Snow Crush

Hang out: Frozen Foods

Corny Cob

Season: Two
ID: 2-004
Rarity: Rare
Finish: Classic
Favorite hobby: Doing puzzles and "maizes."
Shopkins BFF: Poppy Corn
Hang Out: Fruit and Veg

D'Lish Donut

Season: One
ID: 1-035
Rarity: Ultra Rare
Finish: Glitter
Favorite hobby: Playing golf and basketball.
Shopkins BFF: Cheeky Chocolate
Hang Out: Bakery

Freezy Peazy

Season: One

ID: 1-128

Rarity: Special Edition

Finish: Frozen

Favorite hobby: Rapping with my BFFs.

Shopkins BFF: Cheezey-B and Chee-Zee

Hang Out: Frozen Foods

Kooky Cookie

Season: One

ID: 1-039

Rarity: Ultra Rare

Finish: Glitter

Favorite hobby: Acrobatics like somersaulting, and also reading.

Shopkins BFF: Bread Head and Apply Blossom

Hang Out: Bakery

Everybody Loves Toys!

In 2001, a British newspaper called *The Sun* reported that Queen Elizabeth II has a rubber duck in her bathroom that wears an inflatable crown. The duck was spotted by a workman who was repainting her bathroom. The story prompted sales of rubber ducks in the United Kingdom to skyrocket.

Lana Lamp

Season: Two
ID: 2-024
Rarity: Ultra Rare
Finish: Crystal Glitz
Favorite hobby: Reading in bed.
Shopkins BFF: Lisa Litter
Hang out: Homewares

Marsha Mellow

Season: Two

ID: 2-137

Rarity: Limited Edition

Finish: Bling

Favorite hobby: Hanging out around the fire.

Shopkins BFF: Choco Lava

Hang out: Limited Edition

Molly Mops

Season: Two

ID: 2-091

Rarity: Rare

Finish: Classic

Favorite hobby: Playing Mopskotch.

Shopkins BFF: Sweeps

Hang out: Always looking spotless in the Cleaning and Laundry Aisle

Popsi Cool

Season: One

ID: 1-122

Rarity: Special Edition

Finish: Frozen

Favorite hobby: Ice skating.

Shopkins BFF: Cool Cube

Hang out: Frozen Foods

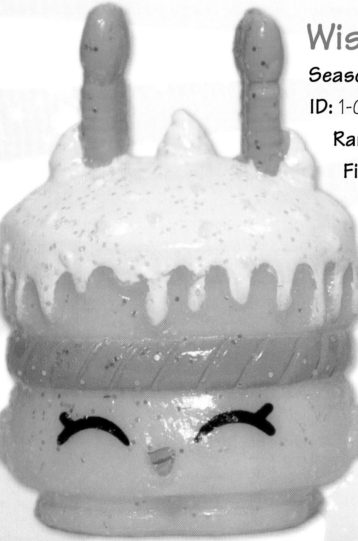

Wishes

Season: One

ID: 1-095

Rarity: Ultra Rare

Finish: Glitter

Favorite hobby: Singing a tune for anyone who'll listen.

Shopkins BFF: Soda Pops

Hang out: Party Section

What Makes Miniatures so Appealing?

Tiny toys have big appeal. Millions of kids — and many adults — are drawn to pint-sized playthings. Shopkins are definitely part of that craze.

Of course, miniatures are hardly new:

- ★ The Tootsietoy brand produced a range of miniature die-cast cars beginning in 1901.
- ★ Wade Whimsies, miniature porcelain figurines measuring about an inch and a half high, were first produced in the mid-1950s.
- ★ N Scale model trains are about the height of two pencils stacked on top of each other. They were first launched by the Arnold Company in 1962.

Dollhouses, with their miniature representations of real home interiors, trace their history back about 400 years to the baby house displays of Europe. While dollhouses are playthings for children, many adults invest enormous amounts of money and time into their miniature dollhouses, filling them with everything from minuscule furniture and curtains to itsy-bitsy plates and glasses. The National Association of Miniature Enthusiasts says U.S. collectors spend upward of $56 million per year on their miniature dollhouses.

So, what's the huge appeal of these tiny toys? Perhaps it's because miniatures allow their owners to easily act out scenes and create stories. Maybe it's because entire collections can be stored in a small box. Or, perhaps it's as simple as the fact that they're easy to transport in a pocket or small bag.

Regardless for the reason behind their popularity, miniatures continue to prove that "sometimes it's the little things that matter most."

chapter four
Lights, Camera, Action

PRODUCTION _Fun at the Beach_

DIRECTOR _Kooky Cookie_

Silly Chilli

CAMERA _____

DATE	SCENE	TAKE
	4	2

Shopkins began posting short animated videos to YouTube in June 2014. The cartoons, all about 90 seconds long, bring these minuscule toys to life.

Created by Moose Toys and animated by Flux Animation Studios, the series is set in Shopville. Australian actress Kate Murphy, a 2008 graduate of the University of Southern Queensland, voices the popular web series. Ross Hastings, whose credits include work on *Bob the Builder*, *Angelina Ballerina*, *Little Charlie Bear* and *Chuggington*, writes the series.

The cartoons are wildly popular and, in less than eight months, have racked up millions of views. The series is fun and entertaining, but it also gives kids a glimpse into the personalities of their favorite characters. It doesn't take long to learn, for example, that Cheeky Chocolate can be an overly confident daredevil, Kooky Cookie is a little shy and very clumsy, and Lippy Lips has a tendency to be bossy.

The series would be boring if the characters just sat on grocery store shelves and looked adorable. Thank goodness the cartoon's creators show favorite Shopkins having adventures, playing, making jokes and even getting in a little bit of trouble.

Here's a quick rundown of the series' first 10 episodes, with view counts:

Create Your Own Shopkins Video

You don't have to own an animation studio to create your own short video starring the Shopkins. In fact, all you really need is an idea, a camera, some Shopkins and some friends.

Start by thinking about the story you want to tell. Are your Shopkins going to visit a new place? Try a new food? Challenge each other in a sporting event?

Figure out which Shopkins you want to star in the video. You may want to ask some friends to help you provide voices and help move the Shopkins as they work their way through the story. You may decide you want to draw backdrops for the different scenes in your story.

Practice the skit several times before you ask a friend or parent to video it for you. Make sure you speak loudly. Practice making different voices for different characters. Do you really think Mandy Candy sounds exactly like Corny Cob?

You can make videos just for your own enjoyment or, with your parents' approval and assistance, you may decide to share them with other Shopkins fans. Go, be creative!

"Check It Out"

Episode Number: 1

Released: June 23, 2014

Views: 2.5 million

Shopkins featured: Cheeky Chocolate, Apple Blossom and Kooky Cookie

"Acting Up"

Episode Number: 2

Released: June 30, 2014

Views: 3.5 million

Shopkins featured: Apple Blossom, Lippy Lips and Strawberry Kiss

"Loud and Unclear"

Episode: 3

Released: July 14, 2014

Views: 1.3 million

Shopkins featured: Cheeky Chocolate, Apple Blossom and Strawberry Kiss

"Choosy"

Episode: 4

Released: August 6, 2014

Views: 1.7 million

Shopkins featured: Apple Blossom, Cheeky Chocolate and Spilt Milk

"Frozen Climbers"

Episode: 5

Released: August 28, 2014

Views: 809,000

Shopkins featured: Cheeky Chocolate, Apple Blossom, Strawberry Kiss, Kooky Cookie

"Chop, Chop"

Episode: 6

Released: September 29, 2014

Views: 776,000

Shopkins featured: Cheeky Chocolate, Apple Blossom and Lippy Lips

"Breaking News"

Episode: 7

Released: October 22, 2014

Views: 529,000

Shopkins featured: Apple Blossom, Cheeky Chocolate, Kooky Cookie, Spilt Milk, Strawberry Kiss and Cheezey Cheese

"Beauty Pageant"

Episode: 8

Released: November 20, 2014

Views: 1.1 million

Shopkins featured: Lippy Lips, Strawberry Kiss, Kooky Cookie, Spilt Milk and Cupcake Queen

The Best Places to Find Shopkins Videos Online

While many online channels feature Shopkins, a few fun channels stand out for their creativity and popularity. Here are the top three YouTube channels where you'll find funny videos showcasing your favorite Shopkins.

Gracie Hunter and her mom, Melissa, are the stars of the YouTube hit **Mommy and Gracie Show**. Together, this mom and daughter duo showcases the toys they love. Shopkins are one of their favorites. Over 100 million people have watched their show episodes! "Our viewers on Mommy and Gracie Show absolutely love Shopkins," explains Melissa Hunter. "They go crazy for our blind bag reveals!" You can find the Mommy and Gracie Show at *youtube.com/user/ MommyandGracieShow*

Cookie Swirl C describes herself as "a girl named Candace who loves bright colors, animals, and just about every kind of toy!" She started her YouTube hit channel Cookie Swirl C in 2014 because she enjoyed making up stories using her favorite toy figurines and sharing them with others. Candace especially loves making videos that showcase her favorite Shopkins. "I hope that my videos inspire you, make you feel creative, and bring you lots of smiles and laughs," shares Candace. You can find Cookie Swirl C online at *youtube.com/ user/CookieSwirlC*

DisneyCarToys is a fun kid-friendly toy channel known for wrapping Shopkins up in colorful Play-Doh®; viewers love watching as the Play-Doh® is unwrapped to reveal a hidden Shopkin. You can find DisneyCarToys at *youtube.com/user/DisneyCarToys*

"Christmas Sing Along"

Episode: 9

Released: December 17, 2014

Views: 2 million

Shopkins featured: Lippy Lips, Apple Blossom, Kooky Cookie, Cheeky Chocolate, Spilt Milk, Strawberry Kiss and Dum Mee Mee

"Pop Goes the Babysitter"

Episode: 10

Released: January 27, 2015

Views: 641,000

Shopkins featured: Dum Mee Mee, Apple Blossom, Strawberry Kiss and Toasty Pop

chapter five

Playing with Your Shopkins

Freezey Peazy, Strawberry Cream and Apple Blossom have taken their places at the starting line. Cheeky Chocolate begins the countdown: "Runners, take your marks. Three, Two, One – GO!"

Freezey surges to an early lead, Strawberry Cream and A.B. are in a close race for second. With the finish line in sight, Apple Blossom lurches forward into a somersault, then another somersault, then another. She's no longer running! Apple Blossom rolls past both Strawberry Cream and Freezey Peazy to win the race. The crowd roars! Sports reporter Slick Breadstick rushes onto the track with his microphone and camera crew, ready to interview the winner.

Runners, take your marks. **Three, Two, One - GO!**

"That was an amazing race," says Slick. "How did you do it?"

After catching her breath, Apple Blossom looks right into the camera and says: "I've always been good in a crunch!"

Yes, it's a silly scene, but it's exactly the kind of fun you can have when you play with your Shopkins.

You can write actual scripts and then use your Shopkins to act them out. You can send your dolls to the supermarket to buy groceries that are loaded with personality. Or, you can really get creative and transform old boxes and fabric into Shopkins beds and houses.

Shopkins board games are coming soon. But until they do, there are plenty of do-it-yourself games you can play with these pint-sized playthings. Here are three great games to play with your Shopkins, whether you have a collection of 10 or 110:

WINNER!

Test Your Shopkins Memory

This is a quiet game for two or more players (or one player and a parent helper). It can be made easier or more difficult by changing the number of toys you include:

Start by placing Shopkins figurines on a tray or baking pan. You might start with 5 to 10 Shopkins for very young players or 15 to 20 Shopkins for older children.

The parent or player who puts the toys on the tray presents it to the other players and allows them to look at the Shopkins for exactly one minute.

Have all players close their eyes while the presenter takes away one Shopkin.

Have all players open their eyes and take turns guessing which Shopkin was removed.

Cuteness Overload

Ask 10 collectors which Shopkins is the cutest and you'll likely get 10 different answers. Our informal poll finds that fans think **Wishes**, a tiny birthday cake complete with candles and drippy frosting, is a true beauty. **Melonie Pips** and **Bun Bun Slipper** took honorary mention in our cuteness survey. Which Shopkins character do you think is most adorable?

Trade roles so that all players have a chance to both guess and present.

To make the game more difficult, you can switch the position of the Shopkins on the tray or remove more than one Shopkin at a time. As a variation, you can have players observe the tray of Shopkins for one minute and then take it away. Each player then has two minutes to write down the names of as many of the Shopkins as they can remember. The person who remembers the most, wins that round of play.

Leapin' Shopkins

Everybody knows that Shopkins love to run and bounce and leap. This activity allows them to fly through the air with the greatest of ease — and it's fun to play by yourself or with a friend.

Begin by using a marker to write numbers on brown lunch bags. You can use any point system and number of bags you want, but here's a great system to start: Use six bags. Write "5" on one bag, "10" on two bags, "20" on two bags, and "30" on the last bag.

Open the bags and set them up in any formation you'd like. A bowling pin-style configuration works great. Then, place a soup can or similar weight in each bag to keep it from tipping over while you play.

Take three big steps back from the bags and create a tossing line. You may want to mark this line with painter's tape or simply make a rule such as, "You can't go past the corner of the sofa."

Each player gets four Shopkins. You can memorize which characters you each have or you could have one player use only Season One characters while the other plays with Season Two. If you have more than two players, you can divide by grocery aisles: Bakery, Fruit and Vegetable, Freezer, Dairy.

Players stand behind the tossing line and take turns trying to toss their Shopkins into the bags. After each player has tossed all four of his Shopkins, use a notepad to see how many points each player earned. If a player, for example, landed Cool Cube in the 20 point bag and Snow Crush in the 5 point bag, he'd earn 25 points for that round.

Keep playing until the first player scores a total of 100 points.

This game can be made easier or more difficult, depending upon how far the players stand from the bags. Very young children may need larger targets, such as full-size grocery bags.

Shopkins in a Bag

This game requires very little preparation and works best with just two or three players.

Start by asking a parent for a pillowcase or small drawstring backpack you can use.

Select 15 to 20 Shopkins from your collection and write their names down on a notepad.

Pecanna Pie

Snow Crush

Toofs

Lippy Lips

Dippy Acacado

Sneak Sue

Cheese Kate

Toffee Coffee

Blossom

Place all the Shopkins inside the bag or pillowcase.

Place checkmarks by five of the Shopkins you know are inside the bag. These are the Shopkins each player will be searching for. The trick is that players must search with their hands — not their eyes. No peeking!

Set the timer for one minute. The first player puts her hands in the bag feels the figurines to find the five she's in search of. When she thinks she's found one, she pulls it out. One point is awarded for each correct Shopkin pulled out of the bag within the one-minute time period.

Figurines are returned to the bag after each one-minute search and players take turns feeling for the right Shopkins. Rounds of play continue until the first player correctly identifies a total of 10 Shopkins.

This game can be turned into a timed challenge for a single player. Using a stopwatch, keep track of how long it takes the player to find all five characters. See if the player can improve her time in subsequent rounds of play. Increase or decrease the number of Shopkins used to make the game easier or more difficult to play. You may also change up which Shopkins players are being searched for or how many Shopkins players need to find.

How to Host a Shopkins Party

Design Your Invitations

Creative invitations set the stage for a fab party. On a small square of paper, print the time, date and location of your party. Tie the paper invite onto a mini Shopkins bag and fill the bag with a brand-new Shopkin. This will give your friend a new Shopkin to start or grow their own collection and get everyone excited for your party!

Decorate!

★ Decorate the party area with festive balloons and streamers that match the colors of your favorite Shopkins: Blue and Pink for D'Lish Donut, Green and Pink for Fairy Crumbs, Orange and Purple for Juicy Orange, etc.

★ Draw pictures of Shopkins onto the balloons that match their colors.

★ Use white craft paper as a table cover. Place crayons on the table to encourage your friends to draw and color their favorite Shopkin.

★ Set a brand-new Shopkin blind bag at each place setting so you can share the fun of opening blind bags and trade Shopkins while you enjoy your cake.

★ Don't forget to set a mini-place setting for your Shopkins!

Goodie Bags

Your friends will go crazy for tiny treasures they can bring home in goodie bags. You can either use a Shopkins shopping bag or shopping basket or decorate some plain lunch bags with colorful pictures of your favorite Shopkins. You can draw them with crayons or markers or cut out pictures from the Shopkins packages. Fill up the goodie bags with a Shopkin, stickers and some sweet candy treats.

Party Games

Shopkins Relay Race

For this game, you'll need two big spoons and four bowls—two empty and two full of Shopkins. Have your guests divide into two teams and stand in two lines. Place the empty bowls on the other side of the room. The object of the game is to carry the Shopkins by spoon, one at a time, from one bowl to the other. The first team to fill the empty bowls with all of their Shopkins wins the game.

To make the game more difficult, give each player a plastic spoon to transport Shopkins – the catch is that players must hold the handles of the spoons in their mouths, not their hands. For another variation, consider having players carry Shopkins using a pair of chopsticks instead of a spoon.

Banana Splitty Race

Use a pen to draw eyes and a smile on a banana, creating your very own Banana Splitty. Give each party guest a banana. Ask each player to place one hand behind their backs, so they only have one hand to hold the banana. The object of the game is to peel the banana using whatever means possible, but using only one hand. The first person to peel the banana and take a bite wins!

Food Fun

★ Why not serve breakfast food instead of lunch or dinner food? Serve up waffles and pancakes with whipped cream for your very own Waffle Sues and Pamela Pancakes. Set up a Breaky Crunch cereal bar with all your favorite breakfast cereals. Add a few drops of pink food coloring to your milk jug, too, to make for a more colorful meal.

★ Make your own Soda Pops by gluing craft eyes and smiles onto small cans of your favorite soda or fizzy fruit juice.

★ Arrange veggie and fruit trays by color to form a rainbow platter.

★ Prepare peanut butter and jelly sandwiches on white bread and use a food safe pen to draw eyes and a smile on each, creating your Fairy Crumbs PBJ Shopkins.

chapter six
Collecting Shopkins

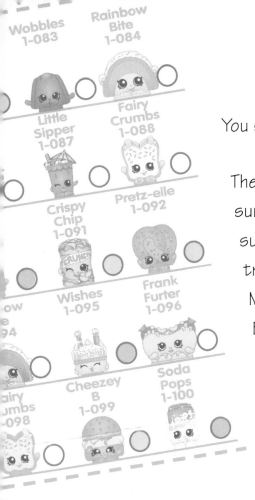

You start with just two Shopkins.

Then you get a 12-pack from a friend. Then Mom surprises you with a 5-pack because you've done such a great job keeping your room clean. Then you trade one Exclusive for three Limited Editions. More gifts, more purchases, more trades … Before you know it, your two little Shopkins will have multiplied to more than 100.

You may not have intended it, but you've become a Shopkins collector.

Shopkins do make collecting easy, thanks to the grocery list-inspired handout that comes with all Shopkins. You can also use the toy's official website, www.shopkinsworld.com, to create "I Have" and "I Want" lists.

There are millions of toy collectors around the world. Some are very, very serious about their hobby, while others just love the thrill of adding to their extensive collections. Some have collections worth millions of dollars; others insist that childhood memories fuel their passion.

Many collectors began collecting toys as kids. Some stop there, while others continue their collections, often refining exactly what it is that they're after.

Toy collector Ricky Philips lives in Leicester, England. He's been interested in toys for more than two decades and now has a collection of around 2,000 action figures. Even with all those toys, he told BBC News in December 2014: "Basically if I like it, I will collect it. I like the hunt, I like to sniff out rare and interesting things and I like to learn more about them."

If you think toy collecting sounds like a fun hobby, you might want to consider these important tips:

Love What You Collect

If Shopkins make you happy, by all means, collect them. They may never be highly sought-after, expensive collectibles – or they may be. Jordan Hembrough, host of the

Amy's Guide

Shopkins Wins Toy World's Highest Honor

Shopkins' Small Mart Playset won the Girl Toy of the Year Award at the Toy of the Year Awards Ceremony in February 2015.

Moose Toys Co-Chief Executive Officer Paul Solomon told *Daily Mail Australia* it was an incredible honor to win in a category generally dominated by toy manufacturing giants.

"It's the ultimate award to win and we're incredibly proud to achieve it," Solomon told the newspaper. "We're up against the powerhouses and the monster entertainment toy giants, so it's a great Australian success story and an enormous feat to bring home."

The award was announced as thousands of toy executives and guests gathered for the American International Toy Fair, an annual toy industry trade show held in mid-February at New York City's Jacob K. Javits Convention Center.

Shopkins' award took on extra meaning because it was voted upon by a cross section of consumers, journalists and bloggers, retailers, and members of the Toy Industry Association.

Work + Play = Success

Shopkins manufacturer Moose Toys has a new corporate headquarters that puts the focus on FUN! The office building, located in Melbourne, has toy testing rooms, a basketball court, whiteboard walls for sketching out ideas, and a tree house-style meeting room located at the top of an oversized beanstalk. Known as "Mooseworld," the new space was designed to inspire employees' creativity.

Travel Channel's *Toy Hunter*, advised *Good Morning America* viewers in December 2012: "Never think of 'what this will be worth down the line.' Collect toys because you love them, not because you think you're going to get rich selling them years from now."

Research Your Hobby

Dig into books, old magazines and websites to learn about toy collecting, the history of toys and the values of toys. Research the specific toy you want to collect. Learn about Moose Toys. When did they first begin making Shopkins? How have they changed? What made them popular? What new toys are planned in the future?

LAUNDRY ★★★

Wendy
Washer
2-089

Bree
Freshner
2-090

Sarah
Softner
2-093

Peta
Plunger
2-094

Squeaky
Clean
2-097

Wendy
Washer
2-098

Sweeps
2-101

Sarah
Softner
2-102

eta
nger
103

Leafy
2-104

SHOES

Sneaky
Sue
2-106

Heels
2-107

Sneaky
Wedge
2-108

Wedgy
Wendy
2-110

Bun Bun
Slipper
2-111

Cute
Boot
2-112

Sneaky
Sue
2-114

Heels
2-115

Sneaky
Wedge
2-116

Wedgy
Wendy
2-118

Bun Bun
Slipper
2-119

Cute
Boot
2-120

BABY

bbles
-121

Ga Ga
Gourmet
2-122

Dum Mee
Mee
2-123

Baby
Swipes
2-124

Baby
Puff

Nappy
Dee
2-127

Shampoo
Sue
2-128

Have a plan

Just saying you want to collect toys is too broad an ambition. It's important to decide on a specific toy line or type of toy. If you decide to collect Shopkins, stick to that goal. Yes, it's great to have a well-rounded, fun toy box, but serious collections need focus.

Watch Your Budget

Collecting toys is so fun that it's easy to find yourself wanting more and more of them. That's great, just be aware of what you can afford to spend. If you get an allowance, you should talk with your parents about what portion of it you can spend on toys.

Always on the Lookout

Toy stores are an obvious place to buy Shopkins for your collection, but they're not the only place to find them. These tiny treasures could turn up at flea markets, swap meets, resale shops, or even at your neighbor's garage sale. You should also let friends know which Shopkins you need to complete your collection because they may be willing to make a trade.

Displaying Your Shopkins

Your parents might freak out when you tell them you'd like to go to a housewares store, but that's truly one of the best places to buy a display rack for your Shopkins collection.

Plastic stair-step spice racks are readily available at housewares and discount stores; most cost $8 to $20. The spice racks typically have three tiers and are designed to organize kitchen cabinets. They also work like risers, so that your Shopkins can have a place of honor in your bedroom.

You can use the rack just as it comes. Or, use one of these ideas to give it some Shopkins-worthy pizzazz:

1. Stickers are the quickest and easiest way to add a burst of color to your display stand. You can use stickers left over from other projects, or you may want to search out a favorite color or even food-inspired stickers.

2. Fabric is another easy way to dress up your display. Start by measuring the height and depth of each step on your tiered rack; add all these measurements up. If the three risers are 1 inch tall and 2 inches deep, you need to add 1+1+1+2+2+2=9 inches; this is the overall height of your rack. Next measure the width of the rack. If the rack is 12 inches wide, you need a piece of fabric that is at least 9 inches by 12 inches. Go to the clearance counter at your local fabric store to find a suitable remnant. A black fabric will add drama to your display case, while a bold print makes a fun statement. Or, perhaps you'll want red velveteen to get a glamorous Red Carpet look. Once you select the fabric, cut it to the exact size you measured — be sure to ask an adult for help. An adult can also help you use fabric glue or a spray adhesive to fasten the fabric to the risers.

3. Make a color photocopy of the grocery list-style handout that comes packaged with all Shopkins. Using scissors, cut the list into rows. Next, cut out the pictures and names of the Shopkins you want to feature. Glue those images to the risers in the spots where you want your favorite Shopkins to stand. You can adhere images directly to the plastic rack or you can use patterned scrapbook paper or wrapping paper to cover the steps first.

You may decide you want to create your own display rack base out of Styrofoam or foam core — especially if you dream of collecting and displaying the entire Shopkins collection. These smaller racks, however, are a terrific way to display and honor your favorites. Get creative! Start displaying!

Most Expensive Toy

A special edition Barbie™ created by Australian jewelry designer Stefano Canturi is reportedly the most expensive toy ever sold. The toy, wearing a black, strapless dress and pink diamond necklace was sold for $302,500 in 2010, with all proceeds going toward breast cancer research.

Care for your Collection

Shopkins are durable, but even the most indestructible toys can be damaged if they're not properly cared for. Extreme heat or cold, for example, can break down plastic, making it brittle. Your Shopkins collection should not be stored on your windowsill because direct sunlight can fade colors in packaging and in the toys themselves.

A Priceless Shopkins

To celebrate the launch of Shopkins Season Three, Moose Toys revealed a priceless, one-of-a-kind character made entirely out of crystal at the 2015 North American International Toy Fair in New York. The crystal Shopkins character, named Gemma Stone, will be auctioned off online later in the year. All proceeds from the auction will benefit the Toy Industry Foundation, a nonprofit organization that distributes toys to underserved, at-risk and homeless children around the world.

Manage Your Collection

Of course, all your toy collecting time can't be spent shopping for new toys. Be sure to make time to play with your Shopkins, re-arrange your displays, clean any figurines that have gotten dirty, and make lists of your favorite or most-wanted figurines. You may also want to keep lists of doubles you own so that you know which Shopkins you may be willing to put on the trading block.

Whether you love the hunt, displaying your finds or simply the sense of accomplishment that comes when you find an elusive Shopkin, collecting should be fun. They are, after all, toys. And toys are meant to be fun!

Toy Museums

While you're busy showcasing your toy collection, others are designing displays on a much larger basis in toy museums. In the United States alone there are more than three dozen toy museums including World's Largest Toy Museum in Branson, Mo., Washington Doll's House and Toy Museum in Washington, D.C., and Kruger Street Toy & Train Museum in Wheeling, W. Va.

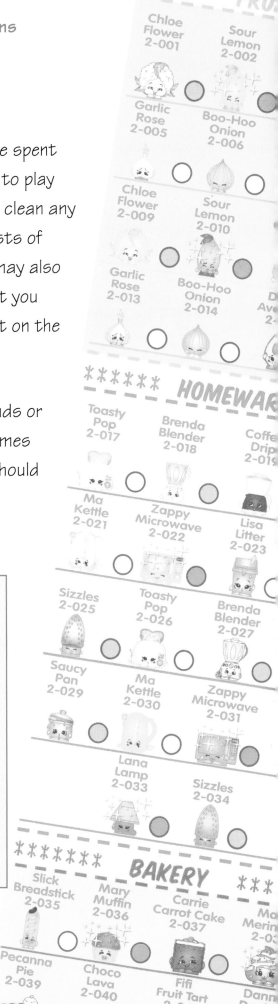

chapter seven
Crafting with Shopkins

Play: It's what Shopkins are designed to do.

But there's even more to these little creatures than fun and games. They're so seriously cute, it makes sense that you might want to include them in some craft projects.

With just a few inexpensive supplies and a little assistance from an adult, you can use your imagination to create some great Shopkins-inspired items for yourself and your friends. These three craft projects are perfect for a rainy day, or you can plan a special craft party with your friends.

Let these projects inspire your own creativity. What other crafts can you make with Shopkins? A mobile? Hair clips? Keychains? Use your resourcefulness and inventiveness to come up with ideas on your own.

No matter what you make, have fun doing it!

Play

It's what Shopkins are designed to do.

BFF Picture Frame

This frame makes a perfect gift for your best friend. Or, the two of you could make them together so you can each have one!

Materials needed:

Unfinished 4-by-6-inch photo frame; acrylic paint; sponge brushes; two Shopkins BFF characters for each frame; paint marker, writer-style paint or permanent marker; permanent craft glue.

Instructions:

1. Cover your work surface with old newspapers to keep things neat.

2. Take the back off and carefully remove the glass from your photo frame. Set these aside while you decorate the front of the frame.

3. Is the photo you're going to frame horizontal (long) or vertical (tall)? You'll want to paint the frame with this in mind.

4. Paint your frame using a small sponge brush and acrylic paint. You can paint any color or combination of colors that you like. Acrylic paint dries quickly. After about 30 minutes, you'll want to give your frame a second coat. Allow the second coat to dry, usually another 30 minutes.

5. If you want to further decorate your frame, this is the time to do it. You can add a coat of glitter paint or add a pattern like dots, hearts or lines. Allow these decorations to dry.

6. When your frame is completely dry, use a paint marker, writer-style paint or permanent marker to write "Best Friends Forever" on the top of the frame. Try to center the words. Let this latest decoration dry so you don't smear the words.

7. Use permanent craft glue to fasten two Shopkins BFFs (such as Mary Meringue and Lippy Lips or Juicy Orange and Sour Lemon) to the lower right and left corners of your frame. Let the glue dry for 24 hours.

8. When everything is dry, put your frame back together – this time showcasing a favorite friend photo. You'll have BFFs on the frame and in the frame!

Best Friends Forever

Shopkins Charms

Transforming Shopkins into charms is super easy. Finished charms can be threaded onto bracelets or necklaces.

Materials needed:

Eye hook screws; Shopkins characters; pencil; cord, hemp, ribbon or ball chain; medium-sized beads, optional.

Instructions:

1. Choose which Shopkins character you'd like to transform into a charm. If you have doubles of a particular character, you may want to use one of those. Or, you may decide this is how you want to showcase a favorite figurine.

2. You'll need one eye hook screw for each charm you're making. Also referred to as screw eye bails, these items can be purchased at a craft store for about $1 for a package of 10 and come in a variety of sizes – 5mm to 10 mm will work best for this project.

3. Locate the top, center spot on your Shopkins character. Use a pencil to mark this point.

4. With an adult's help, screw the eye hook into the Shopkins at the spot you marked. Keep turning the screw until the threads are no longer visible

Amy's Guide

Choco Lava Cupcakes

These delicious mini lava cakes are bursting with hot, gooey chocolate. Top each miniature, lava-filled cake with a swirl of whipped cream and a strawberry, and you've created your very own real-life Choco Lava Shopkins!

> 1 cup of chocolate chips
> 1 stick butter
> 1 teaspoon vanilla extract
> ½ cup sugar
> 3 tablespoons flour
> ¼ teaspoon salt
> 4 eggs
> 12 strawberries
> Whipped cream

Make sure you get some adult help for the mixing and baking part. You can handle the eating!

Instructions
★ Preheat the oven to 350 degrees.
★ Place pretty paper liners in a 12-cup muffin tin.
★ Put a small metal bowl over a saucepan with simmering water. [Be careful, it's hot!] Melt the chocolate and butter in the bowl. Stir in the vanilla.
★ In food processor combine the sugar, flour and salt. [You may want some adult supervision here!]
★ Slowly add the melted chocolate to the food processor mixture.
★ Mix in the eggs one at time, letting each egg get fully mixed before adding the next one.
★ Chill mixture in refrigerator.
★ Spoon mixture into muffin tin. Bake for 10 minutes. The outside of the cake will be cake-like; the center will be gooey.
★ Top each cupcake with a strawberry and a generous amount of whipped cream.

and the "eye" or loop portion of the screw is all that's visible.

5. Thread your charm onto cord, hemp, ribbon or ball chain to create a bracelet or necklace. If you'd like, you can add beads for additional interest.

6. Wear with pride!

Shopkins Magnet Board

You can make Shopkins magnets to hang on the family refrigerator, but this craft takes it a step further by allowing you to create a magnet board for your own room. It's perfect for displaying your Shopkins "Have" and "Want" lists!

Materials:

Cookie sheet or jelly roll pan; pretty scrapbook paper or wallpaper; scissors; double stick tape; six to eight Shopkins; six to eight small disc magnets; permanent craft glue.

Instructions:

1. Start with a cookie sheet or jelly roll pan. These pans come in different sizes; anything will work but a half-sheet (measuring 18-by-13 inches is a really good size). If your family has a pan they no longer use, that

would be great. You can also find these pretty easily at discount stores.

2. Ask an adult to help you measure the flat portion of the pan (where you'd put the cookies if you were using it to bake!) and cut scrapbook paper or wallpaper to fit. Choose a paper color and pattern that will look good in your room. You can use several papers if you want, just be sure to overlap them a little so you don't see a gap between them.

3. Put double stick tape on flat portion of the pan. Don't skimp. Make sure you go all the way around the edges and put some in the middle as well.

4. Carefully press the paper into the pan, smoothing out any bubbles.

5. Next, choose the Shopkins you want to turn into magnets. Fatter, flatter characters, such as Sugar Lump, Cheeky Chocolate and Fairy Crumbs work best for this project.

Adapting to the Times

Toys often evolve over the years. For example, when Mr. Potato Head™ was first released in 1952, the toy included hands, feet, ears, mouths, eyes, noses, hats, eyeglasses, a pipe and hair — but no potato body. The separate plastic parts were to be stuck into a real potato or other vegetable. A plastic potato was added to the kit in 1964.

6. You will need one disc magnet for each Shopkins magnet you want to make. These magnets are available in craft stores and come in a variety of sizes. You'll want to select magnets that are narrower than your Shopkins — half-inch disc magnets are a great size to use.

7. With an adult's help, use a permanent craft glue to fasten the magnets to the Shopkins. Put a dab of glue on each magnet and a dab of glue on each Shopkin. Let the two parts sit for three minutes before pressing the magnets onto the Shopkins.

8. Let the glue dry for 24 hours.

9. When the glue is dry, use your new Shopkins magnets to hold messages in place on your pretty magnetic board.

Storing Your Shopkins

There are organizers and travel cases on the market, specifically designed to store and transport Shopkins and their accessories. These are terrific, but they're not the only way to store your growing collection. Consider these options:

Plastic jewelry storage containers – Used by people who make jewelry, these boxes typically have adjustable compartments. Two other qualities that make them perfect for Shopkins storage? Their lids fasten shut so you won't risk spilling your collection and they're generally made of clear plastic so you can see what's inside without having to open each container.

Small hardware organizer – Most people use these drawer-style organizers to store screws, nails, nuts and bolts. Those same drawers are great for filing mini figurines. The drawers are deep enough you can fit multiple Shopkins in each one, allowing you to have separate spaces for "Party Food" and "Bakery" or "Special Edition" and "Ultra Rare." You might use a labeler to mark the fronts of these drawers.

Tackle box – Fishermen use tackle boxes to carry hooks, bobbers and sinkers. You can use yours to carry your Shopkins. Made of metal or hard plastic, these containers are durable and come with a handle that makes them easy to carry. When you open the boxes, you'll find trays that are divided into tiny Shopkins-sized compartments.

Upcycle a mint tin – Let's face it, if you stick a single Shopkin in your pocket, there's a good chance you might lose it. They are, after all, pretty tiny. Next time you need to transport just one or two Shopkins to a friend's house, use an empty mint tin. Make sure the tin has been washed first. You can use it as it is, or you can decorate your tin with paint or contact paper. Even the tin's interior can be spiffed up with a little glue and some fabric scraps.

These items can, of course, all be purchased new, but they can also commonly be found at yard sales and thrift shops. You might even ask your family and friends if they have a tackle box or hardware organizer they're not using. Just be sure to clean used items thoroughly.

chapter eight

What Do You Know About Shopkins?

You have dozens of Shopkins, you've memorized their names and you've watched all their cartoons at least 10 times. You are a Shopkins expert.

Or, are you?

Think you know everything there is to know about Mandy Candy, Flava Ava, Frank Furter and their friends? These 30 questions will put your knowledge to the test. When you finish, check your answers and see what Shopkins badge you've earned.

25-30 Correct? You're a *Shopkins Master Supreme.* Tiny blue shopping baskets and bags cover your bedroom. You know these toys inside and out, frontward and backward. Well done!

20-25 Correct? You're a *Shopkins Scholar.* You've obviously studied, there were simply questions on the test that you weren't prepared for. Review some more, collect some more, pay attention to the details and try again.

15-20 Correct? You're a *Shopkins Ace.* Your knowledge of these adorable toys is passable but more rigorous play is required. Study session anyone?

Fewer than 15 Correct? You're a *Shopkins Newbie.* There's nothing wrong with that, it just means you need to spend more time playing with and collecting these adorable toys. Get to it!

1. **What type of food is Rainbow Bite?**
    a. Candy
    b. Bundt cake
    c. Kiwi fruit
    d. Cookie

2. **What word is written across the front of Chap-Elli?**
    a. Balm
    b. Lotion
    c. Soft
    d. Fresh

3. **Which of these Shopkins wears glasses?**
    a. Yo-Chi
    b. Frank Furter
    c. Toofs
    d. Bread Head

4. **Which toy company developed Shopkins?**
    a. Mattel
    b. Fisher-Price
    c. Moose Toys
    d. Hasbro

5. **Who is the only Ultra Rare Fruit & Vegetable from Season One?**
   a. Rockin' Broc
   b. Strawberry Kiss
   c. Melonie Pips
   d. Pineapple Crush

6. **Who is Snow Crush's BFF?**
   a. Popsi Cool
   b. Cool Cube
   c. Ice Cream Dream
   d. Pa Pizza

7. **Which of these is not a Category from Season Two?**
   a. Homewares
   b. Health & Beauty
   c. Sweet Treats
   d. Baby

8. **Rub a Glove comes in which finish?**
   a. Classic
   b. Bling
   c. Glitter
   d. Super Glitter

9. Which of these is an actual
    Shopkins playset?
    a. Rub a Dub Shopkins Tub
    b. Cluttered Shopkins Closet
    c. Hot Hot Hot Oven
    d. So Cool Fridge

10. Which of these Shopkins lists
     "writing poetry" as her favorite
     hobby?
     a.   Candy Kisses
     b.   Lolli Poppins
     c.   Jelly B
     d.   Le Quorice

11. Which "team" is Strawberry Cream part of?
     a.   Fruit & Vegetable
     b.   Dairy
     c.   Exclusive
     d.   Party Food

12. Which of these characters
     has a mustache?
     a.   Cornell Mustard
     b.   Al Foil
     c.   Fasta Pasta
     d.   Toasty Pops

13. **Which type of Shopkins are there the fewest of?**

   a.   Limited Edition

   b.   Ultra Rare

   c.   Exclusive

   d.   Special Edition

14. **What is Sizzles?**

   a.   A frying pan

   b.   A waffle maker

   c.   A Deep fryer

   d.   A iron

15. **What does Posh Pear carry?**

   a.   A purse

   b.   A book

   c.   Money

   d.   A flower

16. **Which of these items is not included in the Shopkins Supermarket Playset?**

   a.   Shopping cart

   b.   Delivery chute

   c.   Counter with moveable conveyor belt

   d.   Refrigerator case

Amy's Guide

What's Next for Shopkins?

During the 2014 holiday season, more than 6 million Shopkins characters sold in less than four months, making them one of the hottest collectible toys of the decade. With so many kids excited about Shopkins, it's only natural to see a demand for even more Shopkins-themed fun. Thankfully, the Shopkins family is growing fast!

The newest Shopkins family members are bound to make you hungry. New character packs come in three delicious styles: *Fast Food, Cool & Creamy* and *Cup Cake.* A new Scoops Ice Cream truck will feature a hide-n-find freezer where you can keep your fave icy treats. The all new Shopkins Fashion Boutique has a slide and spinning catwalk, where your favorite fashionista Shopkins can strut their stuff.

Expect to see Shopkins popping up everywhere…in new games, posters, plushies and even school supplies. Shopkins-themed board games, card games, and puzzles are set to launch this year, with posters and plush products and key chains already hitting the shelves of your favorite toy stores. As the chief officer of Moose Toys, the proud producer of Shopkins, explains: "We're all thrilled with the success of Shopkins and the speed with which the brand has taken off in the UK. Shopkins is a fast becoming a licensing phenomenon to match its success in the grocery market!"

17. How many candles are on Wishes, the birthday cake Shopkins?

    a. 1

    b. 2

    c. 3

    d. 4

18. Which of these is not a member of the Shopkins family?

    a. Tin'a'Tuna

    b. Googy

    c. Cinna Mon

    d. Cheese Kate

19. Coolio comes in which two colors?

    a. Green and blue

    b. Pink and yellow

    c. Purple and silver

    d. Pink and blue

20. Who is Breaky Crunch's BFF?

    a. Sugar Lump

    b. Nutty Butter

    c. Googy

    d. Spilt Milk

21. **What color hat does Papa Tomato wear?**
    a.   Green
    b.   Yellow
    c.   White
    d.   Black

22. **Which of these Shopkins is not decorated with sprinkles?**
    a.   Fairy Crumbs
    b.   D'Lish Donut
    c.   Flutter Cake
    d.   Cupcake Queen

23. **Creamy Bun Bun is a kind of pastry known as:**
    a.   Éclair
    b.   Cannoli
    c.   Cream Puff
    d.   Strudel

24. **Which "team" does Nappy Dee belong to?**
    a.   Sweet Treats
    b.   Party Food
    c.   Baby
    d.   Limited Edition

25. **What is Gran Jam's hobby?**
    a. Sewing
    b. Speed walking
    c. Knitting
    d. Making preserves

26. **Which of these characters loves talking on the telephone?**
    a. Cheezey Cheese
    b. Dum Mee Mee
    c. Toasty Pop
    d. Bread Head

27. **What color are the blind bags that Shopkins come packaged in?**
    a. Yellow
    b. Blue
    c. White
    d. Pink

Long Live the Bubbles

Love to blow bubbles on a hot summer day? You're not alone. The folks who know toys best named bubbles to the National Toy Hall of Fame in 2014. The National Museum of Play has honored 41 toys since it opened its Hall of Fame in 1998.

28. Shopkins are from Australia. What other toy comes from Australia?

    a.   LEGOS®

    b.   Barbie™

    c.   The Zelfs™

    d.   Etch A Sketch®

29. Which instrument does Rockin' Broc play?

    a.   Drums

    b.   Guitar

    c.   Saxophone

    d.   Keyboard

30. Which of these Shopkins wears a scarf around her neck?

    a.   Ice Cream Dream

    b.   Cool Cube

    c.   Yo Chi

    d.   Popsi Cool

Answers

1. B; 2. A; 3. D; 4. C; 5. C; 6. A; 7. B; 8. B; 9. D; 10. A; 11. C; 12. A; 13. C; 14. D; 15. A; 16. D; 17. D; 18. C; 19. A; 20. D; 21. B; 22. C; 23. A; 24. C; 25. C; 26. D; 27. A; 28. C; 29. B; 30. D.

chapter nine

The Collectible Club

In the same way that kids today are gaga for Shopkins, earlier generations were drawn to other toys. The Slinky® and Silly Putty®, for example, were top toys of the 1960s, while kids of the '70s put Etch A Sketch® and Rock 'Em Sock 'Em Robots® on their "Most Wanted" lists.

Just because a toy is popular doesn't guarantee it will eventually become a valuable collectible, but it does help. Right now, the market is primed for those who are hunting for toys they had as children. This kind of nostalgia is why the Star Wars™ toys of the 1980s are incredibly popular with collectors.

Many manufacturers have begun marketing certain lines of toys as "Special Collector's Edition." That label could mean that limited quantities of the toy are being manufactured which would make them rare, or it could simply be a label slapped on the box in hopes of selling more toys. Experts stress that, ultimately, the value of any toy is simply what someone is willing to pay for it.

If you think toy collecting might be a fun hobby to try, you should do your research before you start planning your first purchase. Talk to other collectors and visit websites about it to learn about toy values, the best way to store collectibles, and more.

You may decide you want to collect Shopkins or you may be drawn to another toy — there are thousands to choose from! Here, in fact, is information about four of today's hottest toy collectibles:

Counterfeiting Toys?

You've probably heard the term counterfeiting as it applies to money. Some criminals think they can make their own, fake — known as "counterfeit"—money. Those lawbreakers almost always get caught.

But did you know people try to counterfeit toys, too? Counterfeit toys are usually made from low-quality parts and are sold as cheap imitations of the real things. Selling counterfeit toys is a crime. In fact, in 1999 a Minnesota man was sentenced to a year and a half in jail and fined $150,000 for selling counterfeit Beanie Babies®.

Toys on the Big Screen

Everyone loves toys. In fact, people love them so much that they're frequently called upon to star in major motion pictures. It may be only a matter of time before Shopkins star in their own movie. In the meantime, you might want to check out these toy-related flicks:

Toy Story (1995, Pixar) This film follows a group of toys who pretend to be lifeless whenever humans are present, and focuses on the relationship between cowboy doll Woody, astronaut action figure Buzz Lightyear and a young boy named Andy. The movie had two sequels: **Toy Story 2** and **Toy Story 3.**

Toys (1992, Disney) In this movie, a military general inherits a toy company and decides to start making war toys — something that doesn't sit well with his employees. The movie's stars include Robin Williams, LL Cool J and Jamie Foxx.

Small Soldiers (1998, DreamWorks) When a teenage boy buys a set of Commando Elite action figures, he's unaware that they have been programmed with military technology. The toy soldiers spring to life and start taking their orders very seriously.

The Lego® Movie (2014, Warner Brothers) An ordinary LEGO® figurine named Emmet is mistakenly identified as the Special — an extraordinary being with the power to save the world. He's suddenly called upon to work with a team of strangers to try to stop an evil tyrant's plans to conquer the world.

Barbie™

Barbie™, manufactured by the American toy company Mattel®, was launched in March 1959. With more than 50 years of Barbies™ available, they're a favorite of grandmothers, mothers and daughters. In fact, Mattel® estimates there are well over 100,000 avid Barbie™ collectors around the world and that 45 percent of those collectors spend more than $1,000 each year on their dolls.

Vintage Barbie™ dolls from the early years are generally most valuable. The original Barbie™ was sold for $3 in 1959; in February 2015, a mint-condition, boxed pony-tail Barbie™ from 1959 was listed for sale on eBay for $8,499.99.

Recently, Mattel® has sold a wide range of Barbie™ dolls aimed specifically at collectors, including vintage reproductions and Barbies™ portraying characters from TV series and movies, such as *Star Trek*®.

In 2004, Mattel® introduced the Color Tier system for its collector's edition Barbies™. Colors are assigned to the dolls to indicate how many of each model has been produced.

Beanie Babies®

Beanie Babies® were first introduced in January 1994 with nine different beanbag-style animals, including Legs the Frog™, Squealer the Pig™, Spot the Dog™ and Patti the Platypus™. The toys, from Oak Brook, Ill.,-based Ty Inc.®, sold for about $5 each. Over the years, more and more designs were added to the toy line; today there are more than 2,000 different Beanie Babies®.

Beanie Babies® became collectible almost as soon as they first hit the market. Collectors were careful to keep the toys' tags attached and protected by a plastic case (a toy's value is reportedly cut in half if the tag is removed). Real collectors also know that certain qualities make one Beanie® more valuable than another. For example, Beanie Babies® have cloth tags, called "tush tags" sewn into a seam on their rears. If there's a star on the tush tag next to the word TY®, the Beanie® was made in China and isn't rare. If there's no star on the tush tag, there's a better chance that the toy is valuable.

One of the most sought-after Beanies® was first produced in 1997 with proceeds going to the Princess Diana of Wales Memorial Foundation. In February 2015, the auction website eBay featured listings for more than 1,000 Princess™ Beanies®, 12 of which were priced at more than $250,000 each.

Today there are more than 2,000 different Beanie Babies®

Happy Meal® Toys

Happy Meals®, kids' meals sold at the fast-food chain McDonald's™, were first introduced in June 1979. McDonald's™ had given out toys before that, but the Happy Meal® seemed a logical way to continue this giveaway. In the early years, these toys were very simple trinkets, such as balls, erasers, puzzles and Frisbees®. Over time, the toys have become more sophisticated and are often tied to a popular TV show, movie or toy line.

Happy Meal® toys are very popular with collectors. The McDonald's™ Collectors Club isn't officially connected to the restaurant chain, but it does host annual conventions for its 1,000-plus members. Colorado grandmother Carol Lawless is a member of the national

Aussie Terms

Australians speak English but that doesn't mean other English-speakers always know what they're talking about. That's because Aussies have their own distinctive brand of English, full of nicknames and slang.

If you've seen the Shopkins cartoons, you've witnessed this firsthand. The characters often refer to grocery carts as trolleys.

Want to speak Aussie? This list of common grocery-inspired terms will get you started:

Bangers = Link sausage. This term dates back to the early 1900s, when sausages were made with water. When cooked over a hot stove, these sausages tended to explode.

Biscuit = Cookie. Australians love their biscuits. According to food industry experts, the average Australian eats $70.10 worth of biscuits each year, making it one of the biggest biscuit-consuming countries in the world.

Brekkie = Breakfast. Before World War II, the traditional Australian breakfast consisted of grilled steaks and fried eggs. These days, the majority of Australians eat yogurt and toast or commercially produced cereal with milk. Two of the most common cereals are Corn Flakes and a type of biscuit made from wheat, called Weet-bix.

Chook = Chicken. This term was first used back in the 1880s and specifically refers to hens or female chickens.

Crisps = Potato chips. Sure there are plain crisps, but there are flavored ones, too. Some of the most popular crisp flavors in Australia include lime and pepper, sweet chili sauce and sour cream, honey soy chicken, and atomic tomato.

Cut lunch = Packed sandwich. This term can refer to any lunch you'd pack to take to school or work. A sandwich is a popular cut lunch.

Icy block = Popsicle or ice cream bar. Also known as icy poles, these treats are especially popular during Australia's three hottest months, December, January and February.

Reef-n-Beef = Surf and Turf. This is how you might describe a meal that includes both meat and seafood.

Rockmelon = Cantaloupe. Even within Australia, some people use the word Cantaloupe. The term Rockmelon is most often used in Queensland, Western Australia, South Australia and New South Wales.

collector club. "I've been collecting for about 15 years and have every set from then on," she told the (Colorado Springs) Gazette in 2004. "It's kind of addicting. The kids know grandma has Happy Meal® sets they're not allowed to touch."

In the world of collecting, Happy Meal® giveaways are called premiums, not toys. They aren't worth anything unless they're "mint in package" or, as the collectors say, "MIP."

In February 2015, more than 21,000 Happy Meal®-related toys and toy displays were listed for sale on eBay, including: a set of 80, MIP "Furbies"™ (1999) for $899.99; a single MIP "Real Ghostbusters™ Slimer Horn" (1990) for $99.99; and a set of six MIP "The Wizard Of Oz Movie Set 75th Anniversary" figurines (2013) for $89.99.

The McDonald's™ Collector Club has annual conventions for 1,000+ members.

LEGO® Minifigures

Since their introduction in 1978, minifigs have become one of the most popular aspects of the already popular LEGO® brand. These tiny plastic figurines are a hot collector's item, and with high demand comes high prices.

Recognizing how popular minifigs had become, LEGO® introduced its first set of 16 collectible minifigs in 2010. Sealed in plastic bags so that no one could tell what figure was inside, the first set of minifigs included a caveman, a ninja, a robot and a nurse.

Over time, minifigs have become so popular that their inclusion in a particular LEGO® set can make that playset a surefire winner.

In 2013, LEGO®'s collector minifigs, officially known as "Series 10," featured a gold chrome plated figure known as Mr. Gold. Handsome in his top hat and monocle, only 5,000 of these characters were released worldwide. Mr Gold has since become the most valuable LEGO® minifig on the market today, with collectors paying anywhere from $500 to $1,300 for the tiny toy.